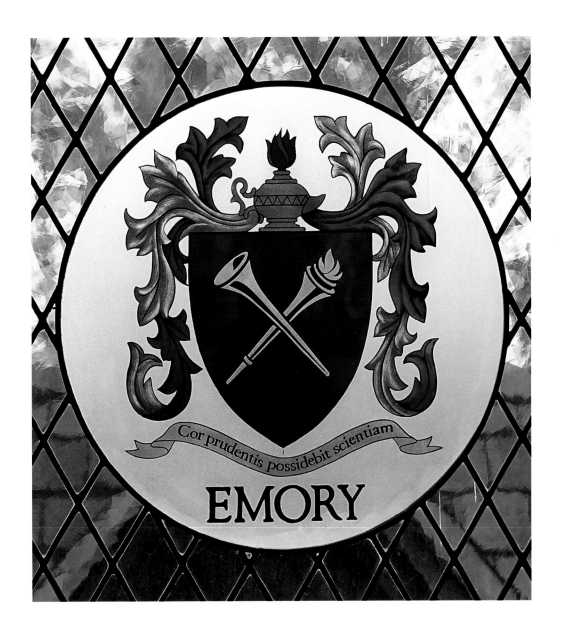

Universities are among the brightest adornments of civilization. Repositories of the accumulated wisdom of civilization, they keep alive [our] noblest dreams and ideals.

Judson C. Ward Jr. '33C–'36G
Emory University Commencement address, 1979

Michael C. Carlos Hall

*The most beautiful building on the campus, with its Roman
arched windows, its pink, white, and blue-tinted marble, its red
tile roof, and its simple Italian entrance—it is a rare example of
architectural beauty.*

The Emory Alumnus, February 1925

EMORY
UNIVERSITY

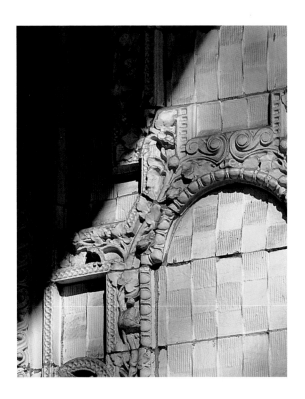

Photography by
William Mercer

Royalston Press
Arlington, Massachusetts

Acknowledgments

We would like to acknowledge the support of President William M. Chace and Senior Vice President of Institutional Advancement William H. Fox '79 PhD.

Vice President for Public Affairs Curt Carlson chaired the editorial advisory board, which comprised Andrew W. M. Beierle, editor of *Emory Magazine* and director of University Periodicals; Ann Borden, director of University Photo/Video; Bruce Burney, director of development for Oxford College; Susan M. Carini, director of University Publications; William H. Fox, senior vice president of Institutional Advancement; Jan Gleason, assistant vice president for University Communications; Gary Hauk, secretary of the University; and Karon Schindler, director of Health Sciences Publications.

In refining the scope and vision of this project, Executive Editor Andrew W. M. Beierle relied on his more than twenty years of experience as editor of *Emory Magazine* and director of University Periodicals. Managing Editor Ann Borden offered nearly two decades of insight into the photographic challenges and opportunities presented by this task and served as Emory's liaison with photographer William Mercer. University Archivist Virginia J. H. Cain proved extraordinarily helpful in researching additional editorial material.

▲▲▲

Dianne Jaquith Schaefer, Designer

Library of Congress Control Number: 2001126957

Hardcover International Standard Book Number: 0-9713382-0-5

First Edition December 2001

Commissioned by Emory University
1380 Oxford Road
Atlanta, Georgia, 30322

William W. Mercer, Executive Editor
Royalston Press
147 Highland Avenue
Arlington, Massachusetts 02476
781-643-4907

Photographs Copyright 2001 by William Mercer

PRINTED IN CHINA

BY PALACE PRESS INTERNATIONAL, SAN FRANCISCO, CALIFORNIA

Film Processing, Color Services, Needham, Massachusetts

Oxford College, Emory's original campus

The Atlanta campus ▶

Architect Henry Hornbostel created order for the campus in two major ways. First, he planned for a spatial order that was created by the main quadrangle, which served as the central focus for the campus. Second, he provided for an aesthetic order through a uniformity of materials and forms.

Architecture/Georgia, Summer 1992

The Quadrangle

*The use of the block form buildings with wide eaves and arched windows
in combination with pink and gray Georgia marble in a random "quilt-like"
pattern suggests the forms of Italian villas and buildings characteristic of
Renaissance Tuscany.*

Nomination form, National Register of Historic Places, November 1, 1973

The Memory of the Place

By President William M. Chace

Human memory, that most fallible instrument, is the only personal means we always have—portable and convenient—that can give us a sense of the past. But the very imperfections of memory leave us with a past that blurs and fades with time. That past becomes corrupted, moreover, by our desire to reconfigure events to our liking. Always available, memory turns out to be a quite unreliable companion.

Certain human inventions do better. Eyewitness accounts, good journalism, video, and the movies can render for us versions of the past that are more dependable than the instrument that always goes with us. But the photograph—still, clear, precise—is best. It gives us stable images, time gone forever but linked to us in a series of still moments: a summer's afternoon in childhood, the look of a grandparent, graduation day, a swelling ocean, the crowded vista of a foreign city, late snow in early spring.

The photograph answers in a fixed way to the moments that memory has ravaged. It retrieves yesterday and holds it firm. And, while having become an art form only in the last century and a half, the photograph has become one of the most popular means of creativity we know. Box cameras, throwaway cameras, digital cameras—all announce our interest in framing moments in time and retaining those moments forever. We use the photograph as a response to what we know are the debilities of memory. Yet a certain kind of danger is present in how we use the camera, the temptation to allow art to introduce its own kind of error and distortion. If we want to recover time gone by, we want accuracy above all.

In this book, the aim of photographer William Mercer has been to refresh our memories of a certain place—Emory University—by means of photographs that are at once faithful to the scene yet aesthetically compelling. The balance he seeks is one between faithful evocation and pleasing result. It is up to every person holding this book (and simultaneously holding memories of Emory) to determine how well he has done, but no one can fail to praise his understanding of light, his attraction to the ways in which color brings us to attention, his delighted discovery of features of the campus that we have seen but have never brought to consciousness.

Asbury Court

Emory University is not only significant as an educational institution but as a physical plant, an architectural complex, a landscape setting, and part of a residential community.

Nomination form, National Register of Historic Places, November 1, 1973

Robinson clock tower on Asbury Circle

What he gives us here is but a very small fraction of the images he captured during his weeks at Emory in the fall and spring of the academic year 2000–2001. He traversed every part of the campus in Atlanta and spent several days on the Oxford campus, where, in 1836, the University began. He saw the world that Emory's 70,000-plus alumni have seen over the years, and he saw it from every plausible angle—from the ground up and from the high reaches of the top floor of the Woodruff Library and the roof of Emory Hospital. Working in time present, he could not recover the distant past for us. This book thus records Emory here and now. (If we want, as we should, to see the Emory of the past, there is now no better source than Gary S. Hauk's superb volume, *A Legacy of Heart and Mind: Emory Since 1836*.) We know that Mercer's book will, as the years go by, also become part of time past, and the images he sets before us in these pages will, some of them, become a record of how Emory "used to be." Certain characteristic features of the University that he has captured, however, will never go out of date: the neo-Classical features of the original architecture that Henry Hornbostel introduced to the Atlanta campus at the turn of the twentieth century; the magnificent trees now preserved as part of campus master planning; the sacred dimensions of the Quad; the marble (quarried in Tate, Georgia) that faces many of the buildings, old and new; and, most importantly, the endlessly enlivening presence of students as they populate the campus and give it meaning as an arena of learning.

University campuses are special places because, from the Middle Ages on, they have been set apart from the busy and hectic world surrounding them. Once gated mini-cities, campuses today still bespeak a separation from the commonplace traffic of the day. They are havens of intellect, reflection, creativity, and reconsideration. Or so they seek to be! But as much as they aspire to turn away from the busyness of the world, the world comes seeking out the intellectual resources that only they can provide. For this reason, Emory has forever been struggling against the forces that, ironically enough, have given it, and will continue to

give it, national and international fame. At the same time that it seeks to preserve the woodlands, the vistas, and the oases of placidity that sustain its internal community, it increases its architectural inventory. Buildings go up and some trees come down.

Hence the world of Emory captured so handsomely in the pages of this book is one in which the old and the new, the hallowed and the innovative, co-exist. The results are sometimes jarring, as witnessed by the conjunction of the two buildings pictured on pages 52–53. This kind of collision reminds us that institutions of the caliber of Emory cannot remain forever the same. As disconcerting as this fact is to the countless affectionate alumni and friends who return to see the place where once they had been, the very nature of learning and research must focus on the future—on what is not now known, yet must be known. Curiosity is at the core of a university's passion and curiosity asks for the means by which its appetite can be satisfied. This dynamism causes new buildings to be built, new laboratories to come into being, new classrooms and lecture halls to replace what once was thought to be good enough.

Emory University today is primarily known as an Atlanta institution, owing to the fact that it was removed, in 1915, from the place of its founding in Oxford,

Georgia, and given a new home on a largely unsettled terrain within the bounds of the state's largest city. Thus, while gaining prominence, Emory also gained a new identity. The Oxford campus remained, however, as part of the University, and its own lovely character is captured in these pages. But one consequence of this dramatic removal is that an institution founded in the early nineteenth century has architecture very much of the twentieth century. That architecture is of its time: nothing quaint, nothing Gothic, much of it clean, rectilinear and functional, and handsomely forceful without being ivy-covered. Such architecture connotes a culture of learning and research that does not look back fondly to the past but forward to new achievement and new intellectual conquests.

William Mercer's photographs, some 140 of them, ask each viewer to reflect on the meaning of a university and its place in our culture. To the question of whether a university is a place primarily for professors or for students, the photographs give support to both propositions: brilliant teaching is displayed here, but so is the energy and promise that only youth can provide. To the question whether a university

Emory University President William M. Chace

is primarily a place that conserves the past or one that looks ahead to the future, the book enters both the archives that make up the library and the laboratories that support scientific discovery. The book shows students both bent to the labors of the mind and flexing every muscle to win athletic contests. The campus is seen at times thronged with the people that give it daily life and, at other times, in moments of unpopulated silence during which the trees and the buildings appear as solitary reminders of what the place is.

But what does remain when the people depart? What is left of a campus when, say, Commencement is over and the graduates file away? After all, universities see people come and go. What remains is memory. Here, to assist memory, to repair its damages, and to prompt every person inspecting these photographs to dwell on the special power and beauty of that unique American invention—the university campus—is a book that also asks us to think about what Emory has been and what it can and must be.

William M. Chace

In a clearing, atop a range of low, thickly wooded hills traversed by
deep ravines is located the remarkable group of buildings which are the
commencement of a great university. . . . These simple, exquisitely colored
buildings along the borders of the forest begirt clearing, are as iridescent
opals deep in a green jewel casket.

The American Architect, October 6, 1920

Staircase, Michael C. Carlos Hall ▶

The degree to which we at Emory succeed in our ambition will depend upon how successful we are in assembling and supporting a community of faculty and students who have the highest possible measure of those traits essential to intellectual excellence: intelligence, curiosity, reason, critical acumen, skepticism, tolerance and openness to new ideas, intellectual integrity, creativity, energy, motivation, and preparation. In the realm of ideas, less than full commitment to those intellectual virtues does not lead to less truth; it leads to no truth at all. This is what justifies our zeal for excellence.

Billy E. Frye '54G–'56 PhD, *A Vision for Emory: Implementing Choices and Responsibility,* 1998

Professor of Chemistry Ronald C. Johnson

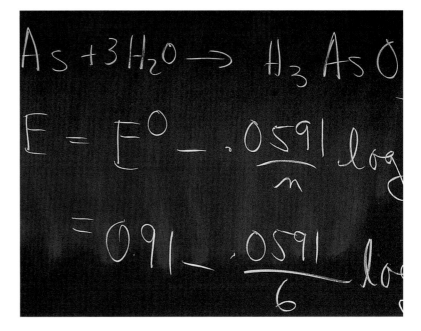

Emory University is not simply a collection of buildings, a place where courses are taught and diplomas are given out. No, the real Emory is much more than these visible signs and activities. The real Emory is, fundamentally, a community of like-minded people, people who have, since 1836, dedicated themselves to certain ideals and maintained certain principles.

John C. Stephens '37C–'38G, Dean of Emory College *Student Handbook* 1965-66.

Loula Walker and Ely Reeves Callaway Sr. Memorial Center

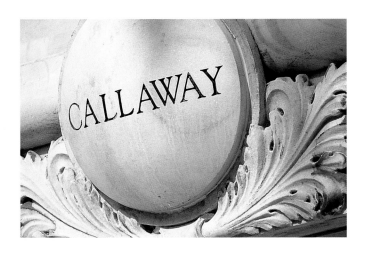

*Visiting architects are struck with
the unusual design of the theological
and law buildings, which deserve
to be numbered among the most
beautiful pieces of university
architecture in America.*

The Emory Alumnus, June 1925

Pitts Theology Library

R. Howard Dobbs University Center

I came to Emory because of the people I met here when I visited. Everyone was friendly and answered my questions honestly.

Emory first-year student

Oxford College dining hall

Alabama Hall

Cox Hall Plaza

Burlington Road performing arts studio

*We envision an academic community that is at once
powerful in its intelligence, moral in its sensibilities, global
in its perspective, and distinctive in its cast.*

Billy E. Frye,'54G–'56 PhD, *A Vision for Emory:
Implementing Choices and Responsibility, 1998*

Oxford College Political Science Professor William Shapiro

Charles Howard Candler Professor of Educational Studies Jacqueline J. Irvine

Williams Gymnasium, Oxford College

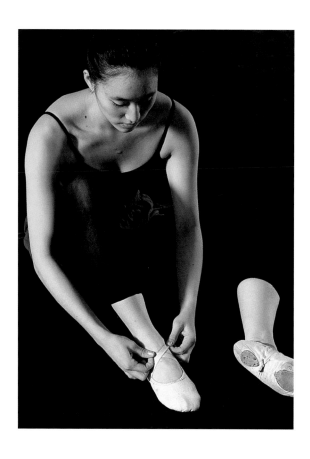

Seney Hall, Oxford College

*A university is first and foremost people, a community
dedicated to pursuing the intellectual life and advancing
understanding of humankind and nature.*

Billy E. Frye, '54G–'56 PhD, *A Vision for Emory:
Implementing Choices and Responsibility, 1998*

Oxford College Rathskellar

My Oxford experience is, in a word, intense. Because the campus, classes, and student body are small, it just seems easier to take the initiative and try new things here.

Oxford sophomore

Professor Eloise Carter and students in a field biology class

Friends stroll the Oxford campus

Oxford College Professor of Physical Education Penny England

Women's soccer at the George W. Woodruff Physical Education Center field

Dooley

"Swoop" and friends

Oxford College

Lullwater House, home of Emory University presidents

Lullwater

*Surrounded by all the natural, radiant beauty of the Emory campus, it is
easier to imagine oneself a hundred miles away from the bustle of the city
life instead of twenty minutes from the heart of Atlanta.*

The Emory Alumnus, November 1924

At the end of all our labors let it be said of the people of Emory that they dedicated themselves to the creation of thought, and that they combined their resources to make mind prevail, to make thinking prevail, to make discovery prevail. If we can do well there, we will have had a triumph never to be forfeited.

Inaugural address of President
William M. Chace, April 5, 1995

Asa Griggs Candler Library

Emory's libraries are so good—there are five of them—and they are connected to the rest of the world's libraries through the web. So basically I have no reason not to get my work done.

School of Nursing junior

Asa Griggs Candler and Robert W. Woodruff libraries

We are a thriving and boisterous institution; take heart every day from that fact. We possess hope and we possess optimism and we possess resolve.

Inaugural address of President William M. Chace, April 5, 1995

54

Men's soccer at the George W. Woodruff Physical Education Center field

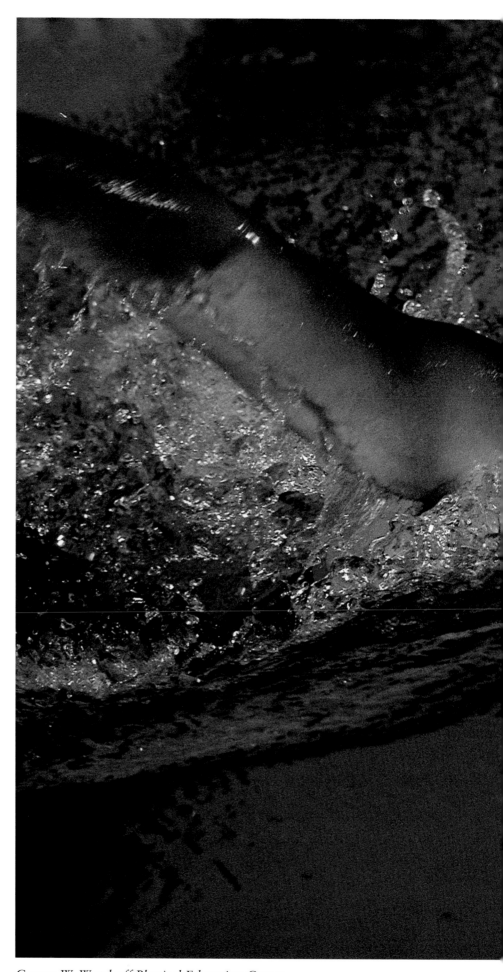

George W. Woodruff Physical Education Center

58

Michael C. Carlos Museum

Robert W. Woodruff Health Sciences Center Administration Building

◄ *Little Chapel in the Glenn United Methodist Church School Building*

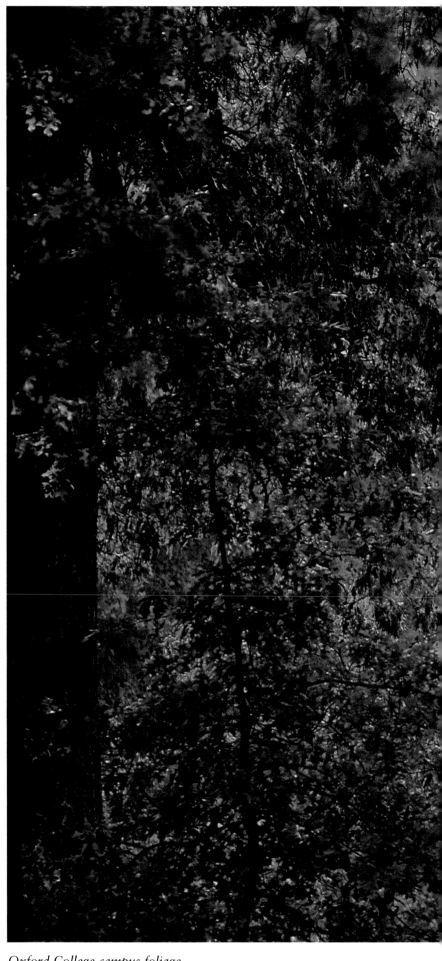

◄ *Seney Hall, Oxford College*

Oxford College campus foliage

Festival of Nine Lessons and Carols

Miller-Ward Alumni House

Haygood-Hopkins Gate

◄ *Glenn Memorial United Methodist Church*

Henry L. Bowden Hall

Henry L. Bowden Hall, detail

Associate Professor of Music William Ransom and student

Cemetery at Oxford College

Pitts Theology Library

Lacrosse at McDonough Field

Baseball at Chappell Park

Track at the George W. Woodruff Physical Education Center

Thus, to all of you at John Portman and Associates, Architects, let me simply say, 'you did it, and you did it magnificently.' Let it be recorded for all posterity that today we dedicate the R. Howard Dobbs University Center with joy, with gratitude, and with much celebration.

William H. Fox, '79 PhD, Dobbs Center
dedication ceremony speech, March 1, 1987

R. Howard Dobbs University Center

Administration Building

Robert W. Woodruff Health Sciences Center Administration Building ▶

Sanford S. Atwood Chemistry Center

Kilgo Circle

Professor of Chemistry Dennis C. Liotta

Michael C. Carlos Museum

William R. Cannon Chapel

Michael C. Carlos Museum

Hugh F. MacMillan Law Library

◄ *Glenn Memorial United Methodist Church*

Hugh F. MacMillan Law Library

Robert W. Woodruff Library

Roberto C. Goizueta Business School

Roberto C. Goizueta Business School, staircase

Emory's location in Atlanta offers the best of both worlds—city life, a green campus, and great weather, too.

Goizueta senior

Howard M. Jenkins Courtyard of the Goizueta Business School

Theater Emory and dance performances at the Mary Gray Munroe Theater

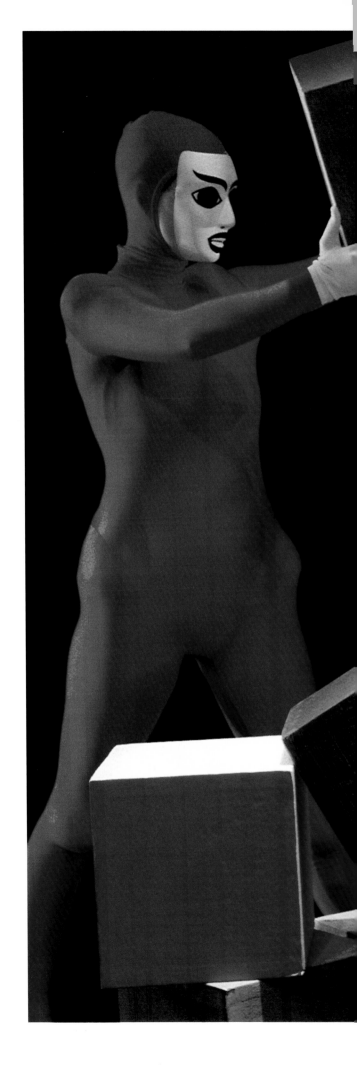

Cox Hall patio

*Each of us must have a place in Emory's life, must have a
sense of ownership, must feel strongly that one is a stakeholder
in the future of this institution.*

Inaugural address of President William M. Chace, April 5, 1995

Atlanta campus

Longstreet Hall

Pedestrian bridge

Nell Hodgson Woodruff School of Nursing, left; and the Grace Crum Rollins Building/Rollins School of Public Health

The story of our school is that of a family tree embracing the Centers for Disease Control and Prevention, Georgia state government, CARE, the American Cancer Society, and many other institutions in the Atlanta community.

James W. Curran, MD, MPH, Rollins School of Public Health dean,
Public Health, summer 2000

O. Wayne Rollins Research Center

Professor of Biochemistry Xiaodong Cheng

Our task at Emory is to uphold the arena of free inquiry while strengthening our sense of who we are as a company of scholars. Now, in this company, I want to affirm that we shall continue to build here, surely and steadily, a university of the first rank. We shall do so by encouraging among us all those qualities of mind and heart and spirit which represent human excellence.

Inaugural address of President James T. Laney, April 13, 1978

W. P. Timmie Professor and Chair of Human Genetics Stephen Warren

Winship Cancer Institute Postdoctoral Fellow Yauhiu Bai

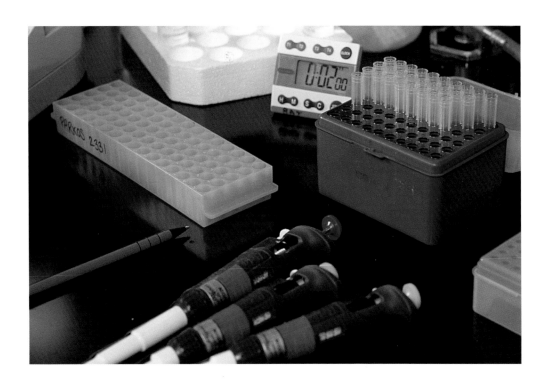

Ben J. Tarbutton Hall, detail

Geosciences Building and Tull Plaza

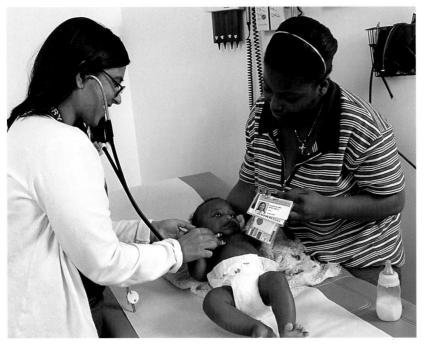

Dr. Neelam Kharod, pediatrics resident, with patient

Our bottom line, our job, and our privilege is to wake up every morning and figure out how to expand young peoples' minds and skills and guide them in their learning.

Michael M.E. Johns, MD,
State of the Health Sciences Center
speech, 1996

Emory University Hospital "H" Wing

Joseph B. Whitehead Research Building under construction ▶

103

There's something very special and good about Emory that attracted me here—a civility, reflectiveness, superb thinkers and leaders, exceptional faculty, staff, and students.

Marla Salmon,
nursing dean,
Momentum, fall 1999

The Robert W. Woodruff Health Sciences Center Administration Building

Harris Hall

Nell Hodgson Woodruff School of Nursing

*Combining two professions—medicine and teaching—into
one brings unsurpassed pleasure.*

J. Willis Hurst, MD, professor of medicine *emeritus,*
Teaching Medicine, 1999

Emory University Hospital

Neuroscience and Behaviorial Biology Laboratory

Robert W. Woodruff Library

110

Let me name immediately the one responsibility that I deem more important than any other: to prize and to sustain a life of the mind that will draw students closer to each other, students and teachers into more powerful associations, and the faculty into a more energetic and enterprising union of intellectual pioneers. Any place so good as this thrives or perishes by how strong its thinking is.

Inaugural address of President William M. Chace, April 5, 1995

Vaccine Research Center

University Orchestra

The first mention of an Emory orchestra appeared in the Phoenix of February, 1887, and some musical organization has been in existence ever since.

A History of Emory University, 1836-1936, by Henry M. Bullock

Emory is a great university, and the Carter Center is a one-of-a-kind institution, and if you bring them together it's going to be a really special place, unlike any other.

Rosalynn Carter, *Emory Magazine*, Autumn 1996

Carter Center of Emory University

Psychology Building

*Dean of Alumni Judson C. "Jake" Ward Jr. '33C–'36G
at the Miller–Ward Alumni House*

*What is important? What is it that endures?
These buildings impress us as beautiful and
permanent. They are but means to education,
not ends, and far from permanent. It is the
spirit of the people who studied and worked
here who made Emory what it is and it is spirit
that will determine its future. Do not be
beguiled into thinking that the physical is
more important than spirit despite the powerful
persuaders of the media to lead you to that
belief. Spirit is what endures, both for
individuals as well as for institutions.*

Judson C. Ward Jr. '33C–'36G
Emory University Commencement address, 1979

Commencement 2000

We are trying at Emory to build a community of character. . . . Emory has sought not just to produce clever people, bright people, technically competent people, but good people. People you would trust. People you would have confidence in. People who have a sense of service for society, who understand what citizenship is all about. People who give of themselves, who understand that real authority comes from giving more than you get.

President James T. Laney,
Board of Visitors meeting, April 23, 1986

*Emory has given me a
lifetime of experiences in
four years.*

Emory senior

Commencement 2000

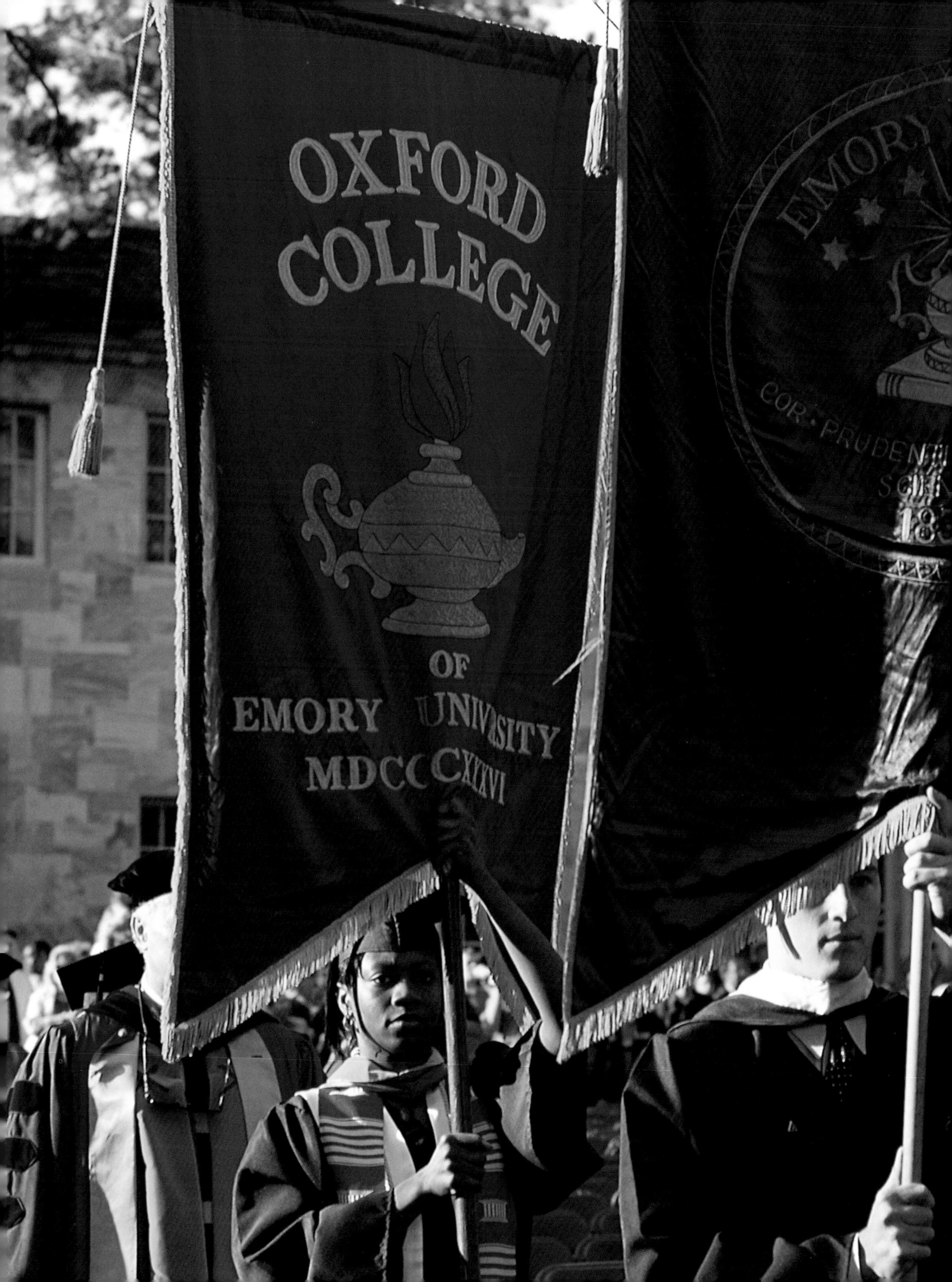
OXFORD COLLEGE
OF
EMORY UNIVERSITY
MDCCCXXXVI

*Emory is being built into finer
proportions and achievement.
That job will never be finished.*

Charles Howard Candler,
Commencement address, 1946

Glenn Memorial United Methodist Church

With the strength we have individually, with the strength we have collectively, and with the strength that our deeply embedded spiritual foundation can give us, let us fasten upon the joy of being at this place. Let everyone have a place amid this bounty. Let us get to work, and be grateful for all the good work we have.

Inaugural address of
President William M. Chace, April 5, 1995